The Cat Family

CHELSEA CLUBHOUSE

An Imprint of Chelsea House Publishers
A Haights Cross Communications Company
Philadelphia

Bev Harvey

This edition first published in 2004 in the United States of America by Chelsea Clubhouse, a division of Chelsea House Publishers and a subsidiary of Haights Cross Communications.

Chelsea Clubhouse
1974 Sproul Road, Suite 400
Broomall, PA 19008-0914

The Chelsea House world wide web address is www.chelseahouse.com

Library of Congress Cataloging-in-Publication Data

Harvey, Bev.
  The cat family / Bev Harvey.
  p. cm. — (Animal families)

  Summary: Simple text compares and contrasts members of the cat family in terms of where they live, body features, eating habits, and size. Species featured include lions, jaguars, tigers, cheetahs, bobcats, pumas, small wild cats, and domestic cats.

  ISBN 0-7910-7541-9
  1. Felidae—Juvenile literature. [1. Cat family (Mammals)] I. Title. II. Series.
  QL737.C23H375 2004
  599.75—dc21

                                                          2002155657

First published in 2003 by
MACMILLAN EDUCATION AUSTRALIA PTY LTD
627 Chapel Street, South Yarra, Australia, 3141

Associated companies and representatives throughout the world.

Copyright © Bev Harvey 2003
Copyright in photographs © individual photographers as credited

Edited by Angelique Campbell-Muir
Page layout by Domenic Lauricella
Photo research by Sarah Saunders

Printed in China

Acknowledgements
The author and the publisher are grateful to the following for permission to reproduce copyright material:

Cover photograph: cheetah, courtesy of Digital Stock.

ANT Photo Library, pp. 4 (bottom), 6 (top), 8–9, 11, 15, 16, 29; Erwin & Peggy Bauer/Auscape, p. 25; Digital Stock, pp. 1, 7 (top); Daniel J. Cox—Oxford Scientific Films/Auscape, pp. 7 (center), 22; François Gohier/Auscape, pp. 7, (bottom), 24; Jean-Michel Labat/Auscape, p. 28; Thierry Montford—BIOS/Auscape, pp. 6 (center), 17; Fritz Polking/Auscape, p. 14; G. Zeisler & Peter Arnold/Auscape, pp. 6 (bottom), 19; Australian Picture Library/Corbis, p. 27; Getty Images, pp. 4 (top), 5, 20, 21, 26; Photolibrary.com, p. 18; Barry Silkstone/Southern Images, p. 23; Michael Wintrip, p. 10.

While every care has been taken to trace and acknowledge copyright, the publisher tenders their apologies for any accidental infringement where copyright has proved untraceable. Where the attempt has been unsuccessful, the publisher welcomes information that would redress the situation.

Contents

Animal Families 4

Where Cats Live 6

Cat Features 8

Cats as Hunters 10

The Size of Cats 12

Lions 14

Jaguars 16

Tigers 18

Cheetahs 20

Bobcats 22

Pumas 24

Cats 26

Pet Cats 28

Common and Scientific Names 30

Glossary 31

Index 32

Animal Families

Scientists group similar kinds of animals together. They call these groups families. The animals that belong to each family share similar features.

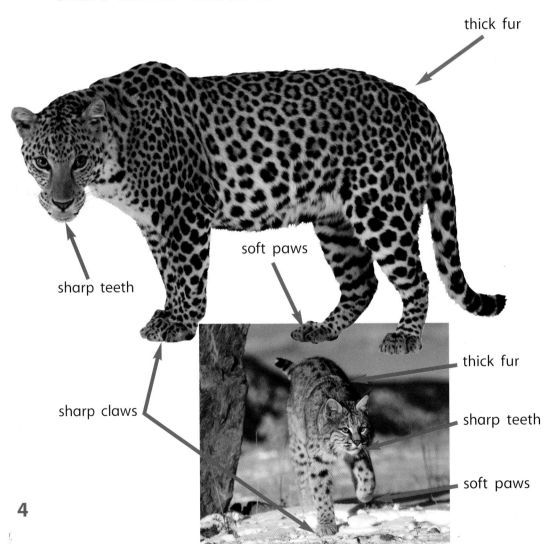

thick fur

soft paws

sharp teeth

sharp claws

thick fur

sharp teeth

soft paws

4

The cat family

All kinds of cats belong to the cat family.
Wild cats live in jungles, on plains, in swamps,
and in deserts. Pet cats live with people.

Cats are a popular pet.

Where Cats Live

Most lions live on the plains of eastern and southern Africa. A few lions are found in the Gir Forest of India.

Jaguars are found in the southwestern United States and south through Central America and South America. They find shelter in forests, shrubby areas, and grasslands.

Tigers live in parts of southern Asia. They are found in places ranging from tropical rain forests in Thailand to cold forests in Russia.

Most cheetahs roam grassy plains in eastern and southern Africa.

Bobcats are found in North America, from southern Canada to southern Mexico. They can live in forests, mountains, swamps, or deserts.

In North America, most pumas live in western regions, though some are found in eastern areas. Pumas are more common in Central America and South America.

Cat Features

Members of the cat family have many features in common.

thick fur to keep it warm

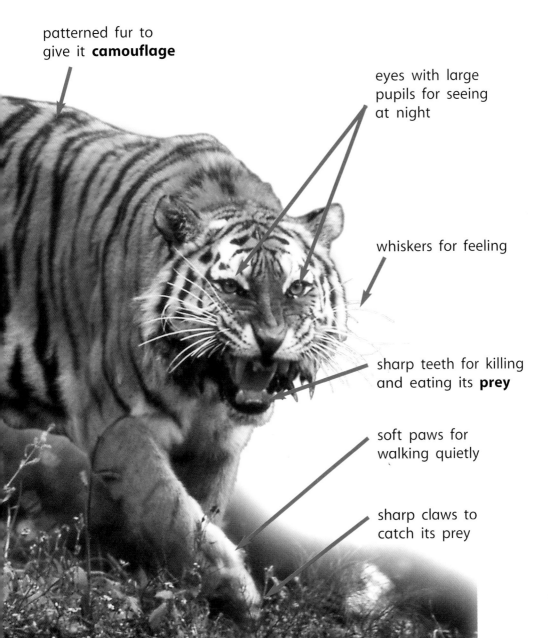

patterned fur to give it **camouflage**

eyes with large pupils for seeing at night

whiskers for feeling

sharp teeth for killing and eating its **prey**

soft paws for walking quietly

sharp claws to catch its prey

9

Cats as Hunters

Cats are good runners and climbers. Some cats hunt at night and some hunt during the day. They can move quietly by walking on the soft pads on their feet.

Cats can see in the dark.

This jaguar caught a fish.

Cats are **carnivores**. They eat meat. Cats **stalk** their prey. When they are close enough, they quickly spring upon and kill their prey.

The Size of Cats

The lion, tiger, cheetah, and jaguar are known as big cats. Big cats can roar. The African wildcat, **domestic** cat, bobcat, and puma are small cats.

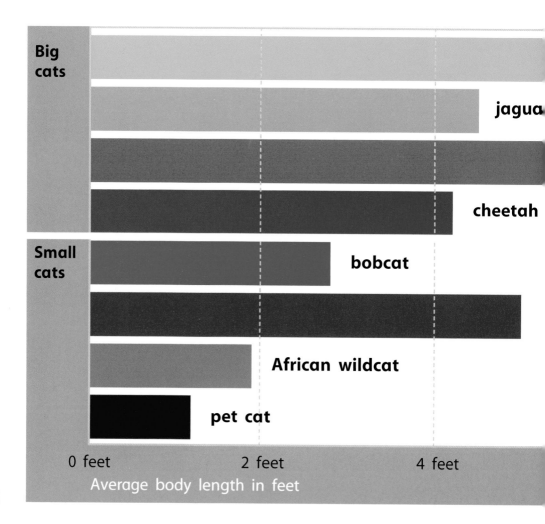

Big cats

jaguar

cheetah

Small cats

bobcat

African wildcat

pet cat

0 feet   2 feet   4 feet

Average body length in feet

Cats are measured from the tip of the nose to the end of the body.

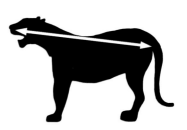

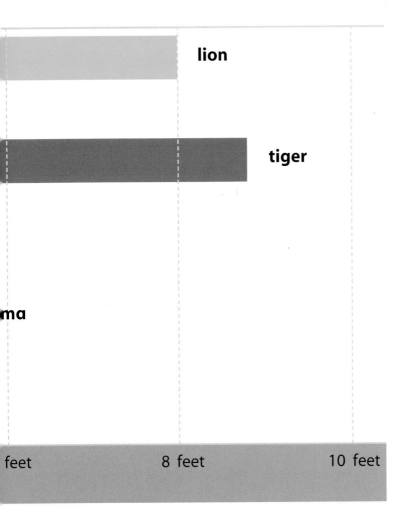

lion

tiger

ma

feet   8 feet   10 feet

Lions

There are two types of lions, African lions and Asiatic lions. Lions live in family groups called prides. The female lion, or lioness, does most of the hunting and caring for her young cubs.

Lionesses work together to catch large prey.

African lions

The African lion is known as the king of the beasts because no other animal hunts it for food. The male lion has a thick, long mane, which makes it look bigger than it really is.

Male lions have a mane of thick fur.

Jaguars

The jaguar is a large, fierce cat. Some jaguars are black, but most have a yellow spotted coat. For many years jaguars have been killed for their fur. Now they are **endangered**.

Jaguars have small dots inside their spots.

Jaguars are good swimmers.

Jaguars live near water. They are strong swimmers and can catch fish while in the water.

Tigers

There are five types of tigers. All tigers have longer back legs than front legs, so they can jump powerfully on their prey. Their strong shoulders and front legs help them to catch and drag down big prey. Their stripes give them camouflage in the long grass.

Tigers are one of the largest members of the cat family.

Bengal tiger

There are only about 4,000 Bengal tigers in the wild. All types of tigers are endangered.

A tiger's stripes give it camouflage.

Cheetahs

The cheetah has solid, black spots. It can run as fast as 71 miles (114 kilometers) an hour. It is the fastest runner of all the cat family. It does not climb trees like the other cats.

The cheetah has a lean body and powerful legs.

Cubs stay with the mother for about 18 months.

A female cheetah will have a litter of two
to four cubs at a time. To protect her cubs,
the mother carries them to a new **den**
every few days.

Bobcats

The bobcat has a short, stumpy tail. Its spotted and striped coat gives it camouflage to hide from **predators**.

Bobcats have pointed ears.

Bobcats have longer hair along the sides of their head.

The bobcat lives alone. It usually sleeps during the day in caves, hollow logs, or in thick bushes. It comes out to hunt at night.

Pumas

Pumas are also called mountain lions.
Pumas are good at climbing trees.

Pumas can climb trees.

Pumas hunt both small and large animals.

The puma is very strong and can leap up to 23 feet (7 meters) in one bound. It usually hunts between dusk and dawn, but it will hunt during the day if it needs to. First it stalks its prey, then it pounces and bites the prey's neck.

Cats

Thousands of years ago, people began to tame wild cats for pets.

People keep cats for company and to control pests such as mice.

African wildcats

The African wildcat is an **ancestor** of the pet cat. Its coat pattern is similar to a tabby cat's coat pattern.

African wildcats are related to today's pet cats.

The African wildcat hunts small prey, like mice and birds, at night. It needs to hunt all night to catch enough food to eat.

Pet Cats

There are many **breeds** of pet cats. Some have long hair and some have short hair. People all over the world keep cats as pets.

Some pet cats have long coats.

Pet cats may still hunt small animals.

A pet cat still has wild **instincts**. If it is turned
loose outside, it may hunt **native** wildlife.

Common and Scientific Names

The scientific name for the cat family is Felidae. There are about 36 types of cats in the cat family. These are the common and scientific names of the ones in this book:

Felidae family			
Common name	**Scientific names:**		
	Genus	**Species**	**Subspecies**
African lion	*Panthera*	*leo*	*krugeri*
jaguar	*Panthera*	*onca*	
Bengal tiger	*Panthera*	*tigris*	*tigris*
cheetah	*Acinonyx*	*jubatus*	
bobcat	*Lynx*	*rufus*	
puma	*Puma*	*concolor*	
African wildcat	*Felis*	*silvestris*	*libyca*
pet cat	*Felis*	*silvestris*	*catus*

Glossary

ancestor	a relation from the past
breeds	types of animals raised by people to look a certain way or to perform certain tasks
camouflage	to blend in with surroundings so it is hard to be seen
carnivores	meat-eating animals
den	a hidden place, such as a cave or a hole under the ground, where an animal lives
domestic	a tame animal that lives with humans
endangered	in danger of becoming extinct, or dying out
genus	the name for a large group of similar animals within an animal family; the genus is the first part of the scientific name of an animal
instincts	a way of behaving that animals are born with
native	an animal species that comes from a particular country
predators	animals that hunt for food
prey	an animal that is hunted for food
species	a group of animals that are closely related and can produce young; the species is the second part of the scientific name of an animal
stalk	to quietly go after prey

Index

b
big cats 12
breed 28

c
camouflage 9, 18, 22
carnivore 11
claws 4, 9
climbing 10, 20, 24
cub 14, 21

d
den 21

e
endangered 16, 19
eyes 9

f
food 11, 15, 17, 27
fur 4, 8, 9, 16, 18, 20,
    22, 27

h
hunting 10, 11, 14, 15,
    17, 18, 23, 25, 27, 29

l
leaping 25
litter 21
long hair 28

m
mane 15

p
paws 4, 9, 10
prey 9, 11, 18, 25, 27
pride 14

r
roar 12
running 20

s
short hair 28
size 12–13
small cats 12
swimming 17

t
tail 22
teeth 4, 9

w
whiskers 9